La Luz del Pueblo

DISCOVERING A SENSE OF PLACE IN SAN MIGUEL DE ALLENDE

LA LUZ DEL PUEBLO

DISCOVERING A SENSE OF PLACE IN SAN MIGUEL DE ALLENDE

PHOTOGRAPHS BY

Jeremy Woodhouse & Nancy Rotenberg

ESSAY BY

Nancy Rotenberg

Luz Books

McKinney, TX

Note on the title:

While our title and the book intend to show the physical light of the town, we also liked this title for its metaphysical implications and connotations suggested in the Spanish. The soul or spirit of the people and the place – *La Luz del Pueblo*.

San Miguel de Allende is a member of the

Organisation des villes du patrimoine mondial
Organization of World Heritage Cities
Organización de las Ciudades del Patrimonio Mundial
Organização das Cidades do Património Mundial
منظمة مدن التراث العالمي
ovpm.org

ISBN: 978-0-615-24691-8

Book Production by Luz Books, McKinney, TX
www.luzbooks.com
Book design by Jeremy Woodhouse
Printed and bound in South Korea

CONTENTS

꧁꧂

San Miguel was founded in 1542, before Zacatecas and Guanajuato came into being. It was created, after a remarkable expedition, by a Franciscan named Fray Juan de San Miguel, who had already created some important Spanish settlements, including those known today as Morelia [1531] and Uruapan [1533].

Up to that time the border of the so called civilized areas of ancient Mexico [Mesoamerica] lay some 80 miles to the south. The Spanish *Conquistadores* needing more land for cattle, began to eye the area north of the Lerma river with interest. These lands were enormous and partially populated by the civilized Otomi Indians who had fled there from the Spanish expansion. But they were also populated by other uncivilized Indians called Chichimecas, who were wanderers and hunters, and uninterested in agriculture. These tribes were inveterate enemies of Aztecs,

Purepechas, and other civilized groups and, of course, were opposed to any European advance.

As usual it was religion which took the lead. Fray Juan, setting out from Michoacán, followed the course of the Laja river northwards. After surviving threats from hostile Indians and the arid nature of the ground he reached a small lake, southwest of the present city of San Miguel, where the Otomies had established a settlement. This he renamed *San Miguel de los Chichimecas* and used it as the springboard for his religious and economic expansions. Time was to reward his actions as silver mines were established in Zacatecas in 1546 and Guanajuato in 1555, which became the richest in the world.

The discovery of silver intensified the Spanish migrations into the Chichimeca area increasing the strategic importance of San Miguel, which was coming under repeated attacks from the

hostile Indians during the period known as the Chichimeca War. In 1555 the Conquistadores weakened, and eventually abolished, the Otomies' influence by refounding San Miguel in a more defendable position near the springs where it lies today, and abandoning the old village.

The rest of the story was inevitable. The Chichimecas were conquered and baptized and the Otomies were subdued. San Miguel became the place where the children of the Spanish who were born in Mexico, the *Criollos* of the 17th and 18th centuries, established a town which was to become of the greatest importance in the fight for independence. Furthermore the *Mexicano* artists of the 1930s onwards came to relish it as a dream of old Spain built with Mexican hands.

Luis Miguel López Alanís
Morelia, Michoacán, August 2008

◄ *Fray Juan de San Miguel and the Parroquia at dusk*

There are those places in the world that cause you to miss your flight home and ask you to consider where home is. There are those places in the world where your face begins to soften and where your soul becomes alive and no longer feels neglected. There are those places in the world where sensual awareness runs amok and where you feel it with every part of your being. As the poet Rumi wrote, you become *'a pearl without a shell, a mindful flooding, candle turned moth, head become empty jar, bird settling nest, love lived.'* For me, San Miguel de Allende is such a place.

As a frequent visitor to bookstore travel sections, I had seen photographs of San Miguel's rainbow-colored adobe structures and geraniums growing out of coffee tins. I had seen quirky skeletons playing guitars and I yearned to visit

the place where artists and lovers, like Frida Kahlo and Diego Rivera received their inspiration. When Jeremy said let's do a photography workshop in San Miguel de Allende, I was packed.

San Miguel is not just a place to visit like a tourist resort. It is a visceral experience where hearts and minds dare to open. San Miguel lives in the experience of senses, not in the mind – it has *sabor* and *ambiente*. Tony Cohan, *On Mexican Time*, writes about San Miguel. *'Here, life is intimate, voluptuous, and sense-driven'*. It is all of that and as a photographer, my mission is to transfer some of that *sabor* into pixels. As workshop leaders, our goal is to help other photographers transfer and record experiences and feelings to their pixels. After half a dozen trips here and many workshops later, Jeremy and I have put this book

together so that you, the reader can enjoy the essence of a wonderful Mexican location, while learning how to approach a town, such as San Miguel, being prepared and ready to photograph a sense of place – *con gusto*.

Que Milagro

As Ansel Adams once wrote, 'We don't make a photograph with just a camera; we bring to the act of photography all the books we have read, the movies we have seen, the music we have heard, the people we have loved.'

It is not enough to show up in a location with a great camera, a good tripod and wonderful optics. To be creative in the photographic process, one must show up in the field – experienced in books, movies and music, and people. One must

◄ *There is a vibrant young population in San Miguel even though it is known as a very desirable place to retire*

bring to the process, not only a map of geographic directions but also a map with a sense of where you are, so that in your discoveries, you will be prepared to really taste and to fully experience life at a deeper level.

I entered into the preparations for my first adventure to San Miguel by visiting my bookshelf, which held books by writers such as Gabriel García Márquez, Julio Cortázar, Carlos Fuentes, Octavio Paz, and Pablo Neruda.

Fuentes said, *'Spanish is the language that with the greatest eloquence and beauty offers the broadest spectrum of the human soul.'* These writers excited me and provided an education of the senses that I would carry with me to San Miguel.

I read Tony Cohan's journey of his time in San Miguel in his two wonderful books, *On Mexican Time* and *Mexican Days*. I revisited Laura Esquivel's *Like Water for Chocolate [Como Agua para Chocolate]*. While the book is a love story between two people, it is also a love story and a metaphor for describing a state of passion, a vibrancy and the sensuality of food for Mexicans.

I read recipes and ingredients in Mexican cookbooks and learned how to say enough Spanish phrases so that I could at least order *pollo* or *pan*, or *vino*, *blanco* or *tinto*. I wanted to communicate if only barely, so that I could ask the cost of something, *cuánto cuesta?*, or good morning, *buenos días*, and certainly the bare minimum respect of *por favor*, *gracias*, and *perdón*.

That was my preparation and certainly, the necessary briefing, but it was not nearly enough to pre-arm me for the magic that I was about to encounter. On my first trip to San Miguel I arrived at night, and after the hour and a half drive from León, I fell into bed, tired from my trip, only to be awakened by what I thought was an invasion of Mexico. In the morning I discovered that this is part of the story here in San Miguel, and the 'invasion' was merely the usual fireworks that occur almost nightly to scare away evil spirits who roam the streets of San Miguel, to declare a birth, to announce a death, to say that someone is going on a journey, or just to celebrate life.

Once I knew that I was indeed safe to go out of the door in the morning, I could not wait to see where I had landed. At once, I was struck by the overload of sensual awareness everywhere and the synesthesia of smells, sounds and sights. Those first breaths actually caused me to stop in my tracks. The air was clear and clean and even on subsequent trips, I have found myself just standing in one place, breathing – both air and fragrances. San Miguel is filled with smells of exotic spices, lavender, rosemary and frangipani. My vision became flooded with the classic Mexican combination of magenta bougainvillea, red geraniums, and violet-blue jacaranda blossoms. The stairways are of vivid colors, rough and smooth exteriors, stone, brick, cement and mosaic. There are stone carvings, exquisitely carved doors and dazzling murals. Clay, papier-mâché, religious artifacts, antiques, both ornate and rustic, *papel picado* banners, colorful oilcloth tablecloths, gardens in bathrooms and varieties of fountains were feasts for the eyes. It seemed endless, and it was difficult for me to stay calm. Everything in San Miguel felt so alive and bursting with energy on that first visit, and it still does – increasing with depth and familiarity whenever I am privileged to visit.

Carrying expensive camera gear has taught me to be wary wherever I travel. I felt very safe in San Miguel – by day or night – and was never hassled or disturbed. In fact, photographing in the *Jardín* and around the streets feels more comfortable than it does in most major cities in the United States or around the world.

Bougainvillea in full bloom softens a stone wall ▶

To really feel San Miguel, you must roam the streets. Suddenly there can be a parade arriving from seemingly nowhere and without warning, people are dancing in the streets. Tony Cohan's words describe this air. *'San Miguel de Allende: site of fiestas and miracles, ecstatic religion and fiery revolt, unearthly beauty and curative air — a place for dreamers and artists.'* Was this a dream or was I just fortunate enough to have arrived in a magical place?

No wonder people fall in love here, I thought. San Miguel must feel like a whirling color vortex. Visitors arrive, often traveling from shades of beige and white — landing in cerulean green, lemon yellow, tomato red, burnt sienna. Words like mango, eggplant, lime and chocolate only begin to describe the intensity and riot of color that washes over everything in San Miguel — and it's all bathed in this glorious light. To be a guest at this very sensual party is indeed a true gift.

La Comida

Like everything else in San Miguel, food is an art form. It is way beyond burritos and tacos and it is sensuous, creative, and savory. It is exactly as Laura Esquivel described. Eating is indeed a love story here.

Some of the concoctions seem to be created from possible ancient earthly mysterious alchemy. Right on the street, you are treated to grilled corn rubbed with lime and sprinkled with chili powder, watermelon juice, *limón* — a small green lime squeezed lovingly over everything. Wherever you go, the *guacamole* and *salsa* are different. The *chiles* are, of course, bountiful, but come in so many varieties and colors that after I learned the difference between *jalapeño*, *poblano*, *habanero*, and *chipotle*, I just ate and enjoyed their delectable flavor — the exception being *habanero* — known by the Mayas as 'crying tongue.' I tried so many varieties of Mexican mole sauce, with mixtures of *tomatillos*, *chiles*, blackberries, and who knows what else. I do know that *mole* should be considered Mexican haute cuisine and viewed as voluptuous and exotic. Many cooks are evasive about their sacred *mole* recipes, sharing them only with family members, and legend has it, that some cooks are so secretive about their sauce components, that they have gone to their graves — never sharing the ingredients. For me, *chocolate y mole negro* is an other-worldly delicacy, and should be experienced slowly to honor all the different layers of flavors. There are combinations of cool salads and hot soups in *pozole*, and *tres leches* cake, which is so ambrosial that it requires you to close your eyes in a dream-like state while relishing, and not question at all.

On that first trip, I experienced two situations that have been imprinted in my mind forever. Sitting under a jacaranda tree, drinking the most amazing hot chocolate, eating a delicious *churro*, reading Carlos Fuentes, I felt this most perfect of feelings. I sensed that I had invited myself to myself and all was good in the world. Moments like this are precious and need to be stored up for those days when a tree is a tree and hot chocolate is merely a drink, and a *churro* is just something that isn't good for you.

The second experience was a response to a woman making corn *tortillas*. I heard the slap-slap sound of her hands flattening the *tortillas* before I saw her. That sound returned me to a root of some sort — possibly one that I didn't know of or one that I had forgotten about. When a person isn't in a hurry and is present, food can be experiential and an incredible nourishment for the soul. Those two experiences are in my San Miguel memory bank to be withdrawn when required. In our busy lives, we often forget about that which feeds us.

◄ *A fine view of the Parroquia from the terrace of local residents John and Diane Patience*

San Miguel food has been influenced by many cultures and traditions – Spanish, French and African. Regardless of what you choose to eat in the vast array of choices, Mexicans are always anxious to share it with you. You are a welcomed guest in any restaurant and so much so that the custom is that restaurant staff will never bring a check unless you ask for it – *la cuenta, por favor*. Can you imagine, nobody pushing you out the door to make room for the next customer!

The markets are a foodie's paradise, with lines and lines of color and exotic variety. Food is rarely pre-packaged, so you will need to bring something to carry home your purchases. Grab a plaid *bolsa* and experience a real connection in buying from someone who has created it, cooked it, fished it, or grown it. This kind of intimate, personal shopping puts passion and juice into the whole experience, and connects me to these souls if only by what is in my *bolsa*. I now use my *bolsa* in North American grocery stores, instead of the offer of plastic bags. San Miguel seems further ahead in the environmental plastic business than we are here in our so-called 'aware' society.

If you love what you've been eating, sign up for one of the many incredible Mexican cooking classes in San Miguel. If you are yearning at home for some wonderful Mexican cuisine and recipes, check out Jim Peyton's web site: www.lomexicano.com. Besides the wealth of culinary information, you can even purchase a flan mold and enjoy the velvet texture of Mexico's most popular dessert at home.

La Persona

'*To live by bread alone*' is generally the lot of the poor, but this does not apply to Mexican folk. Some may lack sufficient food, but nearly always the majority have something beautiful to use – a handsomely hand-woven garment, a lovely pot or bowl. Like their pre-Conquest ancestors, mostly the present-day natives are artists, making objects of great beauty. '*Even the poorest have never completely divorced beauty from utility.*' Frances Toor.

Even with the influx of expatriates to San Miguel, the Mexican soul is the one that weaves its way through the spirit that is Mexico. My experience has been that of a *gringa* and is perhaps affected by a certain feminine sensibility, but these people feel more intimate to me, and very tied to beauty, art, nature and feeling. The intimacy feels much greater than I have grown accustomed to living north of the border.

Particularly on Sunday evenings, you can see families walking together – holding hands. This is not a forced situation – like advertisers try to promote the reasons for families to go on vacation together. This is how it is. They just want to be together. While conversing with a woman on a bench in the *Jardín*, a universal conversation began. She told me of her family in San Miguel, their parties, their dinners, their birthdays. Then it was my turn. 'I live in Pennsylvania', I reported. 'I'm from Toronto, Canada, where many of my family and friends live. My son and daughter-in-law live in Tokyo, my daughter and son-in-law and two grandchildren live in San Diego'. The look on her face was as if I had shared some very bad news. For this Mexican woman, the concept of living apart from those you love was absolutely incomprehensible, and very bad news. 'How do you do it?' she asked. I shared with her that I also find it difficult, but it is the way in The States, and, on many days, I don't know how we do it either.

Mexican people seem possessed of extreme politeness. In watching friends encounter each

◄ *Locals Alex Treviño López and wife Paola Velasco enjoy an afternoon stroll with their son, Silvio*

other, there are many exchanges of greetings, handshakes, pleasantries, and an almost ritualistic back and forthness. In passing on the street, there is always a greeting of some sort. You do well, as a visitor, to learn the basics of *buenos días*, *buenas tardes*, and *buenas noches*. In a crowd, it is expected that you say *con permiso* for excuse me, and of course, *gracias* is said often, and is always welcome.

My experience has been that Mexicans live in pride of their courageous survival, are steeped in a treasury of Mexican folklore of myths and tales, and are warm, generous, and seem to believe that their lives should contain zest and humor. In San Miguel, there is patience and kindness when you are photographing. Sometimes people wait in their cars or on foot until you see that they are waiting and tell them thank you, or when they see that you are finished and start to pack up your gear. There are no stop signs in San Miguel, and drivers have learned to be polite and considerate – perhaps out of survival. San Miguel was inscribed as an UNESCO World Heritage site in July 2008 and no traffic lights are allowed in the city centre. There is little road rage in a city of almost 100,000 and there are few accidents. This is pretty incredible given the lack of lights.

Even with the *alto* or stop signs outside the city, I have noticed that few drivers stop. This does seem strangely appropriate to me, as this country would not exist if they had paid attention to all of the stop signs along the way.

There is a very strong sense of community here. Perhaps it is that people actually use their feet on the narrow streets that were originally created for *burros* or horses. Perhaps because they walk and live at a slower pace, it gives them time and opportunity to talk to people, to be more intimate, to be so human. Perhaps it is their love of *fiesta* and mysticism that brings them together for so many occasions and traditions. It is not just the Mexicans who have created a sense of community. The expatriates have found a shelter here and they seem pleased with their choice. When they pick up their yoga mat, or enroll in a Spanish class, they seem inspired to live their lives in the poetry that runs through this entire town.

Mexicans have incredibly interesting faces and of course, their faces are the subjects of much interest for photographers. I would learn to ask permission – *puedo tomar una foto?* May I take a photo? While this may not gain you permission, you have at least shown yourself to be a polite visitor. Some Mexicans will object to having their photograph taken. At first, I thought that it was the philosophic concern that a photo might steal your spirit. While this is true when considering some Native American cultures, the indigenous people of San Miguel are concerned that *gringos* will make big money from those photographs — either from paintings or publication in magazines and books.

Jeremy and I set up model shoots for the workshops and we pay our models a sitting fee. That feels like fair business trade. If I'm attracted to a vendor as a possible subject, I feel good about purchasing what they are selling. It seems like a good exchange and although I have quite the doll collection as a result of this, I will always enjoy purchasing their wares and then asking for a couple of photographs.

If it's a *fiesta* or parade, I view photography as similar to journalism privacy laws. If people place themselves into the public eye, they have chosen to give up their privacy. Mexico is a culture stretching back many hundreds of years and often in parades and such, Mexicans are so proud of their costumes and of themselves that they will happily pose for a picture. Digital photography

The portrait tells much about the spirit and gentleness of a culture ▶

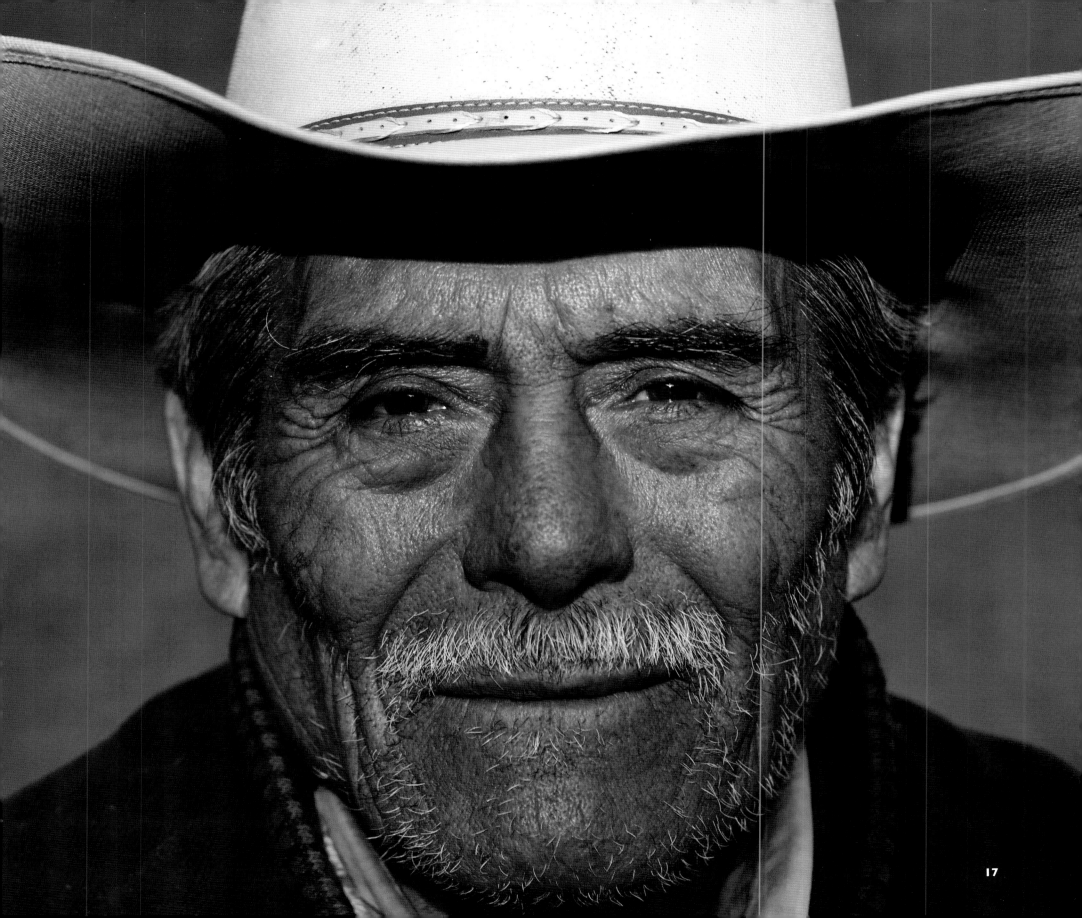

has really helped as people seem thrilled to see themselves in the instant replay on your LCD, creating confidence that you are earnest about capturing them in a polite, honorable manner.

On Mexican Time

The *mañana* philosophy is not as exasperating as I would have thought. In a way, it is very liberating. Days operate in San Miguel but not with the efficiency that we aspire to in the States. For me, this is almost a relief from a lifestyle that is often mechanized. There is a simplicity and a correctness in not being in a hurry. The philosophy is that things get done or not – or there must be a good reason. This leaves time to chat, time to walk, time to be.

It's funny though since things can change on a dime – or I guess, on a *peso*. As Mary Ellen Songer says; '…*in Mexico, the earth is not quiet.*' Everything could change at any minute and it often does. Magic could happen around the corner and I've seen it.

A morning might bring an unexpected parade, an art show, a dance in the *Jardín*. There might be an encounter with someone who is so interesting that it takes you into lunch and then an afternoon discussion. Going into the *Jardín* for morning light can bring a photo bonanza of reflections as the cleaning staff water the walkways – revealing buildings, flowers, people, sky – all reflected in beautiful morning light in the puddles on the cobblestones. Walking around the corner, there can be an elderly lady tucked into a doorway selling flowers or a man with hats piled on his head. It is never quiet, never predictable, and almost never the same.

There is *mañana*, which is a good thing because there is so much to do. San Miguel is a place where the architecture, the riot of color, arts, and produce are a feast for the eyes. You need time to explore and enjoy Mexican art and the many appealing handicrafts. Mexican art reflects a people's love of creating and decorating. This love is seen everywhere in the folk art but also in textiles and embroidery, ceramics, jewelry, and mask making.

A glance into the San Miguel Events Calendar on www.portalsanmiguel.com will reveal where in one week [for example, May 18-24], you could participate in art shows, dance salons, house and garden tours, traditional indigenous oral tales and legends, films and live theater and concerts, writers' and readers' forums, walking tours, mysteries of the Enneagram, community choir practice, discussions on the philosophy of life, dream interpretations, cooking classes, bilingual conversation classes, wine tasting, bingo benefits SMA Red Cross, *milonga* – tango nights, chess, singles mixer, klezmer and gypsy music, meditation shambala, disco adult night, computer obedience training, eating disorder discussions, gay nights, bereavement groups, weight watchers, yoga in the park, a rubber of bridge, backgammon and AA meetings. You could be busy every minute or be busy – merely being. Portal San Miguel will also let you know about the many fine restaurants, what's happening at the art institutions like *Bellas Artes* and the academic information for the *Instituto Allende*. There is news about shopping, real estate, excursions, and anything else that you might like to know about being on Mexican time in San Miguel.

El Jardín

The *Plaza Principal*, the *Jardín*, is like a community living room. The stew of people relaxing on the iron benches or milling about the vendors could be from a Fellini movie. They are old, young, multi-generational, Europeans, Mexicans, expats, cowboys. There are costumes, designer clothes, masks, boots, bare feet, hats of all sorts, and vendors of all sorts. There are women in *rebozos*, often with a baby tucked securely in the folds, dogs of all shapes and sizes, pigeons, balloons and toys. There is a rhythm and stream of people who flow to the vortex of the *Jardín*. They gather, mingle, and connect. The sharing here is the thread that weaves through this whole San Miguel tapestry, and even on a cool winter day, the coming together of it all, is warming to the soul.

In the *Jardín*, the whole town is centered around the three hundred year old, fantasy-like, pink, gothic cathedral. Designed by Seferino Gutierrez, the cathedral, known as *La Parroquia*, is also called the Church of St. Michael the Archangel, patron saint of San Miguel. In evening light, the *Parroquia's* sandcastle spires or 'wedding cake' as it is sometimes known, unfolds in pigments of pink and rose. Usually, the lights of the cathedral are turned on as twilight enters San Miguel, and it is quite a dramatic spectacle. Any photographer worth his salt is sure to return home with spectacular photographs of this wonderful structure.

Live music may start up at any time on the streets. You could hear a wooden xylophone and enjoy some marimba or trumpeters, violinists, guitarists, and a singer or two from a *mariachi* band. There are out-of-tune guitar pickers and an accordion or harmonica that might appear. Foreign rock acts were not allowed to play in Mexico until the late 1980s but now foreign music can be heard everywhere and often.

There is free entertainment in the plaza ranging from *fiestas*, to dancing 10-foot tall papier mâché *mojigangas*. There are comic routines and sometimes as many as a dozen *mariachi* bands that roam the *Jardín* looking for any appreciative audience. What they lack in tunefulness, they make up for in passion. In the words of Jake and Rocket, the founders of 'Life is Good' t-shirts, *'Remember, the music is not in the guitar'*.

Whatever post-party mess which might occur in the *Jardín*, the next morning will bring clean-up squads in orange jumpsuits with wispy, twig brooms, ready to make it 'right' for the next party. I observed them one morning, while photographing a blue trumpet vine against a stucco wall. A hummingbird dropped in and seemed to be in sync with the rhythm of the sweeping brooms. Already in these morning hours, I was treated to yet another dance in the vibrant energy that runs amok in the *Jardín*.

La Fiesta

San Miguel is a town that loves to celebrate. Mexicans often say, *'somos muy fiesteros'*, we enjoy a good celebration. This is evident in their calendar filled with ceremonies and *fiestas*. There are so many festivals and sometimes you only hear about them by word of mouth or via firework bursts. There is The Blessing of the Animals, the cowboys and the horses, *Cristo de la Conquista*, *San Patricio*, *Fiesta de la Santa Cruz*, *Corpus Christi*, *Fiestas Patrias*, *San Miguel Arcángel*, *Fiesta* of St. Michael, Running of the Bulls, and various surprise festivals and events that seem to magically appear.

As a photographer, always be ready. I have developed the habit of having one camera around my neck, ready to go, as I got tired of being late while fussing with gear, and missing fleeting opportunities. Don't be surprised to turn a corner and discover brilliantly hued tropical bird feathers arranged in dazzling ensembles on head-dresses, in the dance of the quetzals. Be ready for unannounced clowns, masks, drums and flutes,

The Fountain at Casa Luna Pila Seca decked out with Christmas poincettias [la flor de noche buena] ▶

a band dressed in regional outfits, or a dressed up donkey or two. It is really incredible, and for me, it is part of the *milagro* that is San Miguel.

Cinco de Mayo holds great cultural and historic significance as it is the chance to reflect on the value of freedom and the courage of a people that, as underdogs, and against all odds, held on to a belief and to their country. Interestingly, *Cinco de Mayo* is celebrated more in the United States than in Mexico. Perhaps it is important for the Mexicans who have moved there, to hold on to their roots and to their core.

Christmas brings parties and celebrations with processions, symbolizing Mary and Joseph's journey to Bethlehem. Poinsettias have become known as *la flor de nochebuena*, the flower of Christmas Eve, and are everywhere around San Miguel. Traditional *luminarias* are constructed – paper bags filled with sand and a lit candle. All *fiestas* in Mexico are organized around food, and Christmas is no exception – especially the *tamale* feasts. *Feliz Navidad*.

The more important celebrations are Lent and Easter and Day of the Dead. Lent and Easter are the spring messages of rebirth and of religious rites. *Semana Santa* is a week long celebration that is so revered many employers simply close down their businesses. *Cascarones*, decorated party eggs are often filled with confetti and broken over people's heads, and are a part of the festivities. Two Sundays before Easter, a procession of thousands of pilgrims arrives in San Miguel after an all-night, 10-mile pilgrimage from the Sanctuary of Atotonilco.

Día de los Muertos, Day of the Dead, has its origins in the belief of the pre-Hispanic Tarasco people of Michoacán. It is believed that the dead could return to their homes on one day each year. Grounds are covered with orange marigold petals or chamomile or wheat, or sometimes with boughs of red gladiolas. The marigold, the *cempasúchil*, is said to be the flower of the dead with its aromatic scent set out to attract the souls and draw them to the offering prepared in their honor. There are elaborate altars, *ofrendas*, sometimes containing large photographs of the person, personal mementos of food, a special sweet bread called *pan de muertos*, sugar figures, candied fruits, *mole*, *tamales*, *enchiladas*, and what-ever drink the deceased might have enjoyed. There are sometimes music and bands, hired to accompany the gathering of family and friends.

Day of the Dead is a community experience but at its core, it is a private, family reunion.

Although it is a wonderful experience to witness a culture that so honors and remembers its dead, it was really difficult for me to take photographs. The gatherings seemed like such personal experiences and I felt rude and intrusive. Whenever I did photograph, I was sure to thank them for the privilege, and remained as polite and respectful as possible.

Death is not to be feared in this culture. It is just viewed as part of the continuing cycle of life. The skeleton, the *calavera*, is the key symbol for Day of the Dead. The *calavera* are not meant to be morbid or frightening. They are merely a part of life's cycle. *Calaveras* can be whimsical – they can be playing guitars, carrying flowers, dancing, laughing. One sweet little calavera sits on my night table and reminds me of this tradition and of the importance of life's continuance, and to always remember to celebrate life.

Octavio Paz writes: *'Fiestas are our sole luxury. They are a substitute for, and perhaps have the advantage over theatre and vacations, Anglo Saxon weekend and cocktail parties, bourgeois receptions and the Mediterranean café...'*

◄ *The calavera, or skeleton, is a key symbol for Day of the Dead*

La Arquitectura

San Miguel de Allende is a blend of old and new and most honor the old and work to keep it in good shape. There are tranquil, welcoming spaces that incorporate nature into their design. There are palettes of reds, pinks. ochres and blues. Hand-painted *Talavera* tile is everywhere, as are ornate wrought-iron gates.

Murals, decorating Mexican walls are works of art. They are eclectic in range with religious origin, patriotic leanings, and color and nature. There are private oases, cloistered behind high walls, and in the décor, there are always flowers.

Mexico is home to more than 25,000 species of plants and every region is filled with avid gardeners. Even the most humble of abodes, has a geranium or a lily in a coffee tin or plastic glass.

Casa Luna Pila Seca and Casa Luna Quebrada are the villas that we stay in whenever we visit San Miguel. Diane Kushner, with her incredible sense of taste and flair, has filled these two architectural works of art with bougainvillea, Virginia creeper, philodendron, ceramic pots, folk art collections, amazing kitchen delights — all allowing visitors to really feel immersed in Mexican flavor. Writing about Diane's villas makes me drift off into a dreamlike state — surrounded by all that she adds to the San Miguel experience.

The cobblestones and rugged sidewalks have given San Miguel a reputation of being 'the city of fallen women' but I'm not sure that this is why they fall. They might fall because they are so busy looking and seeing at all that there is to offer. They might fall because being in San Miguel is like falling in love — where you are at once distracted, enamored and engrossed. I see San Miguel as a falling-in-love relationship as it acts as a mirror reflecting me back to me. I observe myself open and blossom and respond to its energy and its life. It is a love relationship that remains dormant until I return to dissolve into its arms and become a butterfly enjoying the flowers of its soul.

My house is filled with Mexican mementos and many varieties of folk art. I sleep under a bedspread of *huipiles*. I have *rebozos* of every color hanging on an armoire. When touching their handmade embroidery, I marvel at the incredible combination of color and textile. My favorite clothing and jewelry are those that I have purchased in the *mercado* or from local artists.

I leave San Miguel and can't wait to return. Each time there is this renewal — there is this feeling of coming home. Perhaps it is the sun that warms my bones or the colors set out like veritable banquets. Perhaps it is the courage that Mexicans have shown over the years and the hopes of dreams fulfilled. Whatever the reason, my soul is nourished, and I return and return — *con gusto*.

San Miguel has left its mark and I wait to revisit — *con amor y besos y abrazos*. On returning from Oz, Dorothy said, *'but it wasn't a dream, it was a place.'* Yes, San Miguel is a place and it is to be enjoyed like a wonderful dream.

Nancy Rotenberg
Pennsylvania, August 2008

The courtyard of Casa Luna Quebrada ▶

LA LUZ EN LA CIUDAD

[Light in the City]

'Where does a trip begin?
Where does the first idea come from?
But then, where does
a love, a friendship, begin?'

Paul Morand, Voyage to Mexico

'…don't deprive yourself of the experience
by being focused on the final product. Eat, walk, talk and shop.
Art is not only a noun.
Art can be a verb — a state of being.'

Nancy Rotenberg

▲ *Early morning is about the only time that it is possible to photograph in the streets free from traffic and parked cars.*

Cual es el valor de la prisa? [What's the rush?]

Anon — Seen on a bumper sticker

'There are
no
foreign lands.
It is the
traveler only
who is
foreign.'

Robert Louis Stevenson

◄ *The 'photographic moment' is transient. This reflection of the convent bell tower [left] was photographed in a puddle in the cobblestones. The next day the hole had been filled in! The recently painted Parroquia looms softly in the backround of this closeup image of one of the bells [above].*

A good traveler sees what he sees,
the tourist sees what he has come to see.

G. K. Chesterton

▲ *Flags made in the traditional* papel picado *craft style are widely used during times of* fiesta.

◄ *Early morning [left] and late afternoon light [right] has a special quality which enhances the warm, earthtones of the city.*

'A detail

is quite capable

of eliciting

a greater intensity

of emotion

than the

whole scene

evoked

in the first place.'

Eliot Porter

▶ When photographing in the city, dawn and dusk are great times to be out. There is a small window when artificial light will be balanced with the ambient light, such as in this image of the church of Las Monjas.

▶ This image, taken soon after, shows what happens when there is not perfect balance between the different light sources – the subtle colors on the church's dome have disappeared into silhouette and the lights have started to burn out. There is, however, good balance in the overall scene.

Good balance is maintained between the ambient light and the artificial light, with the added bonus of a pink boost from light reflected off the clouds.

Without the added kick from light reflected off the clouds, this image, taken a few minutes later, has a cooler feel. The light balance is close to perfect with detail showing in some of the deepest shadows.

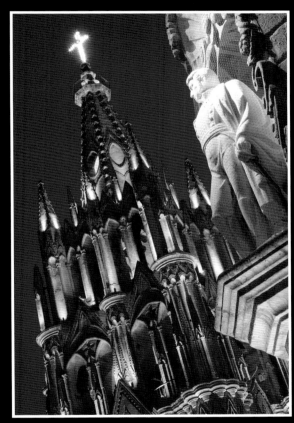

▲ *Steps leading up to the second floor of the Bellas Artes Building [left]. Pedro Martinez painted this mural in 1940 in the style made famous by Diego Rivera. A local artist captures a morning scene in pastels [right page].*

TORTILLERIA

43.

To hold the detail inside the Tortilleria [left] I shot this image twice, first exposing for the exterior, and then for the interior. The two images were then combined in Photoshop. Unfortunately, the Tortilleria, once on Calle Insurgentes, just down the street from the Bar San Miguel [right], has been replaced by a parking garage!

Dusk and dawn are magical times for photography. Light can be almost spiritual,

This nine-frame, stitched panoramic image shows the statue of local hero, General Allende, the centerpiece of Plaza Civica General Ignacio Allende.

◄ *When on location, keep an eye open for hidden gems. If you can gain access to private residences or hotels, there may be new opportunities,*

not always available to the tourist in the street. The images on this spread were photographed in the beautifully landscaped gardens of the exclusive,

Casa de Sierra Nevada.

LA LUZ DEL PUEBLO

[Spirit of the People]

'Embark on the journey with your whole being, experiencing your wish to grow and evolve'.

Federico Garcia Lorca said '*I am tied to the land, in all my emotions.*' To go beyond documentation with your images, to really interpret where you are, the photographer must be more than just a tourist. To photograph intimately, you must visit the interior courtyards – the tiny chambers of both yourself and your environment. To photograph a destination in a mindful way, you must develop a mindful way of seeing, where you are giving attention to architecture, people, color, food, texture, poetry, trees, music, light and religion. Noticing requires a careful attention to listening, to style, to life and death.

When Jeremy and I first visited San Miguel, we were both prepared for a town that is so much more than enchiladas, rice & beans and margaritas. I had read Diana Kennedy, often referred to as 'the high priestess of Mexican cooking', and was ready for the art form that Mexican cooking truly is. I learned what a brightly woven *huipile* looked like and was looking forward to trying mango sprinkled with chili power. Even my limited research about Pancho Villa allowed me a greater understanding of a culture where revolutions inspired revolutions and why Mexico has such a complex legend. The more knowledge you acquire before you leave home, the more your level of understanding will bring greater depth to your photography.

Real growth in your adventure will occur if you remain open, flexible and committed to the philosophy that your ordinary life can be transformed and realized in an extraordinary way. Embark on the journey with your whole being, experiencing your wish to grow and evolve. Enter without preconceived notions, bringing attention and appreciation to the possibility of amazing gifts.

— *Nancy Rotenberg*

▲ *Dancers from the Danza Azteca Quetzalcoatl troupe entertain tourists in the Jardin in a colorful and energetic display which goes on for hours.*

The Conchero Dancers, as they are also known, sometimes reach a state of self-hypnosis, enabling them to dance for hours without apparent exhaustion.

[This spread and following spread].

▲ *There is a low-key security presence in the center of town in the form of mounted police [Caballeria Turística] dressed in traditional uniforms. They are happy to pose for photographs [right].*

To mark the beginning of Semana Santa, or Holy Week, thousands of pilgrims [left] make the all-night, torch-lit walk from the holy shrine of Atotonilco to the Church of San Antonio Abad in San Miguel carrying the statue of Nuestro Señor de la Columna, a life-size replica of a bleeding Christ.

'What I thought was the dead had come back to life.

I realized that while I had believed that I was walking over a cemetery of a culture,

the culture had been abiding beneath my feet.'

Carlos Fuentes

◄ November 1, All Saints Day, and November 2, All Souls Day are marked throughout Mexico by a plethora of intriguing customs that vary widely according to the ethnic roots of each region. Common to all, however, are colorful adornments and lively reunions at family burial plots, the preparation of special foods, offerings laid out for the departed on commemorative altars, and religious rites that are likely to include noisy fireworks. November 1 is usually set aside for remembrance of deceased infants and children, often referred to as angelitos [little angels]. Those who have died as adults are honored on November 2.

Dale Hoyt Palfrey

'The Mexican is
familiar with death,
jokes about it,
caresses it,
sleeps with it,
celebrates it;
it is one of his favorite
toys and his most
steadfast love.'

Octavio Paz
The Labyrinth of Solitude
Grove Press 1961

'Que maravilloso sera cuando este dolor que nos destroza el corazón

se torne de alegria y podamos jugar.'

Anon — Inscription on a memorial in the San Juan de Dios Cemetery, San Miguel de Allende

'How marvelous it will be when the pain that is eating away at our hearts turns to joy and we can play.'

'You can dance anywhere,

even if only in your heart.'

Unknown

'He who sings scares away his woes.'

Cervantes

'At the still point of the

turning world…

there is only the dance.'

T. S. Eliot

◄ *A quick visit to a local tango dance studio resulted in our hiring two dancers, Gonzalo Julian Gonzales Flores and Renata Tagel to come and pose for a group of eager photographers. [this spread and the following spread].*

'There is only one
moment when a picture
is there,
and an instant later
it is gone forever.
My memory is full of
those images that
were lost.'

Margaret Bourke-White

'the decisive moment, it is the
simultaneous recognition, in a fraction
of a second, of the significance of an
event as well as the precise organization
of forms which gives that event
its proper expression.'

Henri Cartier-Bresson

The famous 'Martha' of Martha Shoes [left]. The iconic San Miguel shoe was especially designed for walking on cobblestones and is a 'must' for comfort and style. The 'hat man' carries stock on his head [right] and Señor Hemeregildo poses for photographers during a model shoot [right page].

▲ *These images of incredible local faces were converted to black & white using the Photoshop technique described on page 176.*

The images on this spread show the difference between a portrait taken in direct sun [left] and one in bright overcast conditions [this page]. The image photographed in the softer light shows more detail whereas the other shows more texture.

DÉTALLES GRÁFICOS

[Graphic Details]

Once you have found an interesting subject look for alternative images by changing your perspective or by using a different lens — revisit the location and photograph it in different light. Be bold and unapologetic about your image-making. If someone criticizes you for framing a building with a horse's rear end, why should you care? Argue for your vision and for your voice in the creative process.

I'm always captured by visual design. When I discovered the lines and shapes and color of these lanterns and the juxtaposition of the walls, I was excited. Compositions which contain strong elements of visual design contain impact.

◄ *Inspired by Nancy's image [left page], I returned to the scene at a different time of the day and put my own 'spin' on it giving it a dynamic diagonal composition. I particularly liked the lantern in silhouette.*

'The faculty of
creating is never given to us
all by itself.
It always goes hand-in-hand
with the gift
of observation
and the true creator may
be recognized
by his ability to find about him,
in the commonest and
humblest thing,
items worthy of note'

Igor Stravinsky

'If you do not see
what is around you every day,
what will you see when you
go to Tangiers?'

Freeman Patterson

'A good traveler

has no fixed plans,

and is not intent

on arriving'

Lao Tzu

'The most important thing is
not clicking the shutter...
it is clicking with the subject.'

Alfred Eisenstadt

There is a common photographic adage that says that the best time to photograph a horizontal is after a vertical. This is especially true if you are going to market your work. Having both orientations in your image collection gives an editor a choice and increases your chances of a sale.

DISEÑO Y COLOR

[Design & Color]

'Going beyond the handshake' is a term that we utilize when we explore the options beyond the initial greeting. In this way we develop a deeper relationship with our subject. We are always on the lookout for different ways to describe subjects. Reflections in water, in windows and in puddles, provide such a venue for going 'beyond the handshake'. In traveling the extra mile we begin to create metaphors. Thus a documentary subject is transformed into a more interpretive image. In many ways, this is writing poetry with our photography.

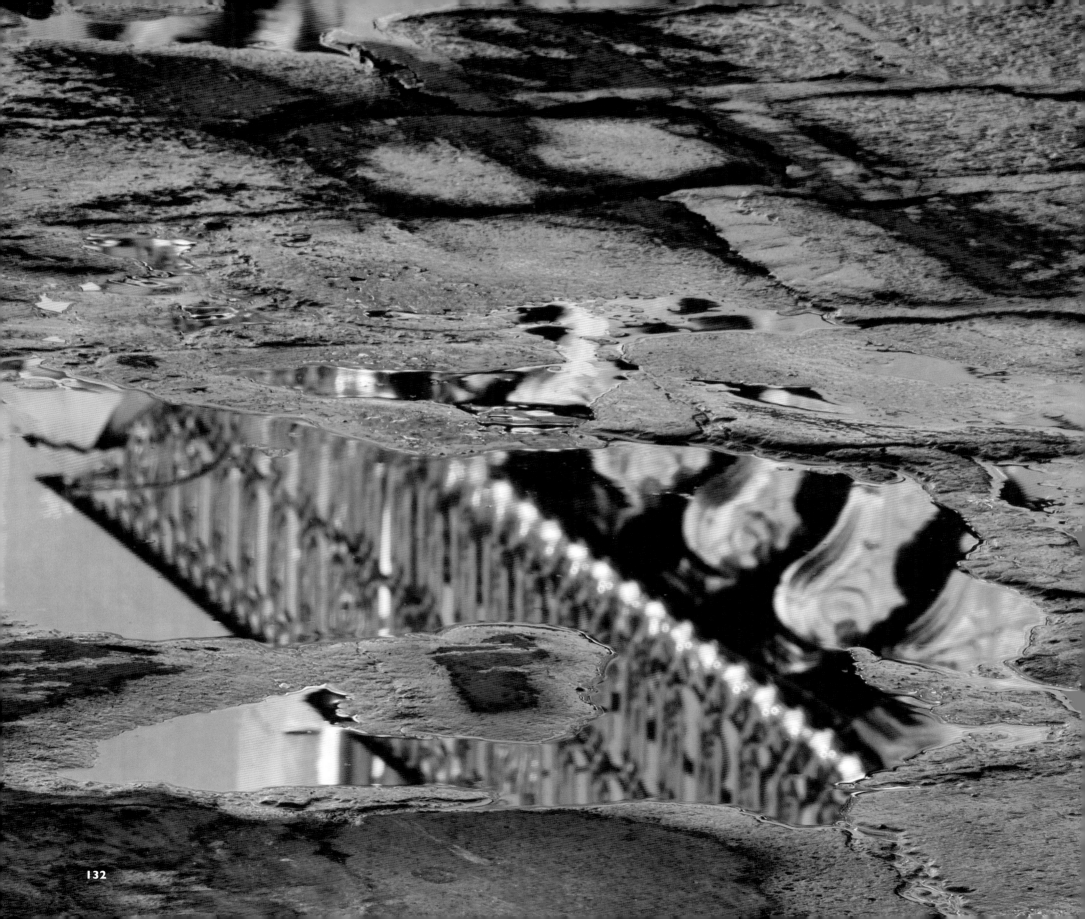

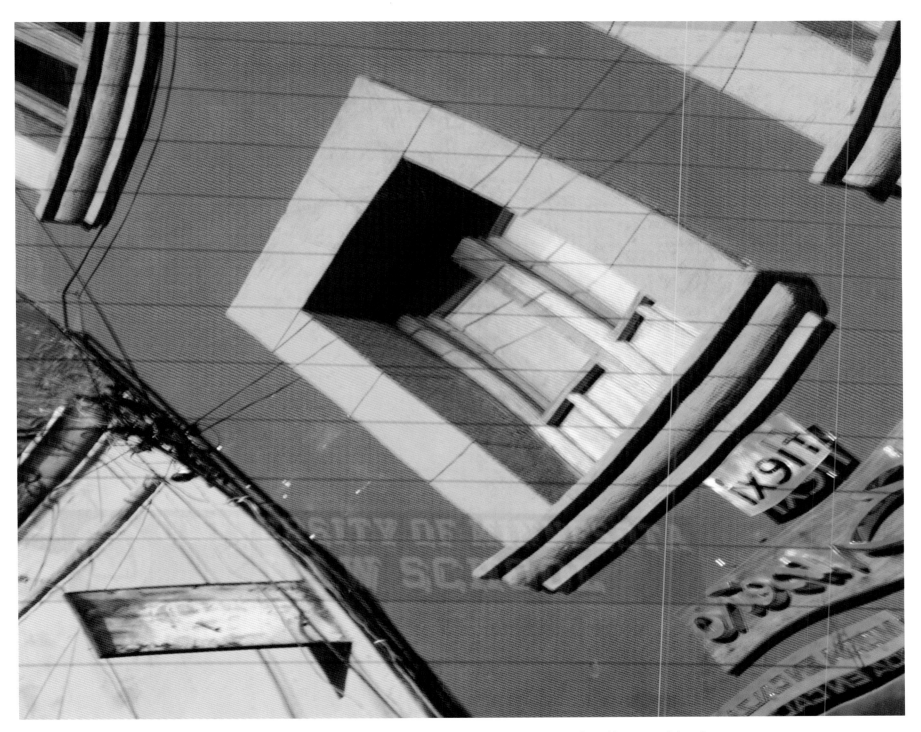

◄ *Reflections are everywhere, whether in a puddle in the cobblestones [left], or the back window of a car from Minnesota [above].*

139

'When confirmed shoppers die and go to heaven,
they may well find themselves in Mexico.'

Steve Rogers and Tina Rosa
The Shoppers' Guide to Mexico

◄ *For the past several years we have held our workshops at Casa Luna B&B. Diane Kushner, with her incredible sense of taste, has filled these two architectural works of art with bougainvillea, Virginia creeper, philodendron, ceramic pots, folk art collections, amazing kitchen delights — all allowing visitors to really feel immersed in Mexican flavor [p. 148-151].*

This whimsical home belonging to celebrated San Miguel artist, Anado McLauchlin and his partner Richard Schultz, is a feast of color and a treasure trove of traditional Mexican folk art, mosaics, textures, and counter-culture artefacts. Anado and Richard live in a gallery of beauty – exemplifying Mexican flair.

159

TÉCNICAS DIGITALES

[Digital Techniques]

1. *Processing with Adobe Camera RAW*

Unless you are a sports or a news photographer, or speed of delivery is important, you would be encouraged to capture your images in the RAW format. Unlike the JPG format, RAW images retain all of the original data captured on exposure. The RAW file is your digital negative and, when processed through a RAW converter such as Adobe Camera RAW, you have complete control over the processing, whereas JPG captures go through some in-camera optimization, as well as destructive compression on saving the file.

RAW files can be captured in16-bit mode [in reality this is around 14-bit] which essentially records tens of thousands of shades of gray in each of the R, G & B channels resulting in a possible palette of billions of colors. JPG files can only be captured in the 8-bit mode which records 256 levels of gray in the R, G & B channels, resulting in a possible palette of 16.7 million colors [to determine this multiply the levels of gray for each channel together – 256x256x256=16.7 million].

This may seem to be a trivial argument for choosing the format you will use, but in the days of film we never compromised on the quality of our film – we always opted for the richest colors and the finest grain possible – so why, in the digital era, when we have more control over the quality of our images than ever before, would we now start to compromise the quality of our digital captures?

The following is intended to be a simple introduction to the world of RAW processing – a starting point for those of you who have still not made the switch.

There are various RAW converters – my RAW converter of choice is Adobe's Camera RAW and the following project was performed using Adobe Camera RAW v4.5 and Adobe Photoshop CS3.

USING CAMERA RAW

To launch Camera RAW double click on a RAW image [one that ends in .CR2 Canon and .NEF Nikon] and a dialog box will open [Fig 1]. The first thing to do is to set up some basic parameters which will then become your defaults.

At the bottom of the screen there will be a blue hyperlink, select this and the 'Workflow Options' box will open [Fig 2]. Select Adobe RGB1998 as the color space [make sure your camera's space is the same]. The color depth should be 16 bit. The native size of your camera's output will be the default [in this case a 12 megapixel camera which will produce 36 MB RGB files – multiplying the megapixel size by 3 will give you the final file size in megabytes]. If you need a larger file you can opt to interpolate at this stage in Camera RAW or resize the image later in Photoshop. If you choose to resize here select the pop up box and choose the new interpolated size Set the resolution to the value that suits your final output

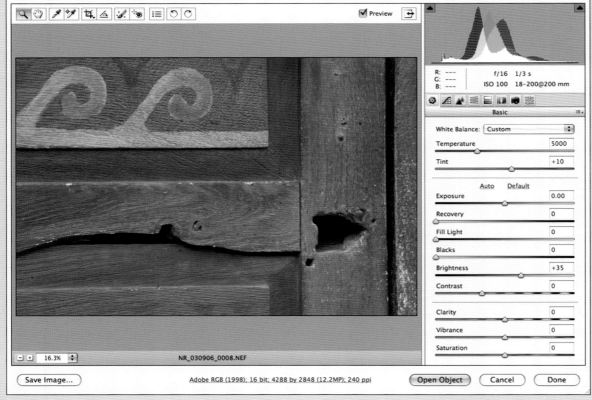

Fig 1

Fig 2

device [inkjet output 200dpi, 4-color process 300dpi, screen resolution 72dpi] – my stock agents require files with a resolution of 300dpi so I opt to change that setting here.

Once you have made these changes use Fig 1 as a guide for your default settings. These are the settings that work for me, and depending on the lighting conditions of my images I make further changes accordingly. The last change I make is to select the 'Tone Curve' icon next to the 'Basic Settings' icon at the top of the right hand section of the dialog box [Fig 3]. Select the 'Point' tab and then set the 'Medium Contrast' option for the tone curve. This helps the image to look a little less flat, a characteristic of RAW files.

At this stage save these settings as your defaults. Select the small menu icon to the right of the heading 'Basic' and select the option to 'Save New Camera RAW Defaults' [Fig4].

Before I begin to optimize this image in Camera RAW let's look at the basic settings and see what they do.

Fig 3

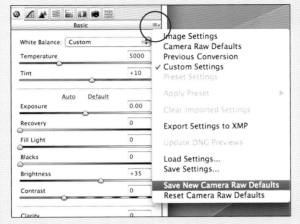

Fig 4

CAMERA RAW SETTINGS

▶ *Temperature* controls how cool or warm an image will be. Daylight temperature is around 5,000 Kelvin [my default]. Moving the slider to the left will cool images which are over warm, and moving the slider to the right will warm images shot in 'cool' situations such as in shade – equivalent to using a 81A warming filter with film. You may opt to have the white balance setting in Camera RAW reflect the 'As Shot' mode. I choose not to and make my adjustments from my 'neutral' default settings.

▶ *Tint* controls the magenta/green shift. My default of 10M seems to work for me most of the time.

▶ *Exposure* works in exactly same way that it does on a camera [there is a 3-stop range in both under and over exposure]. The secret here is to use the histogram to make sure there is no over or under exposure in the image. This is also called 'clipping', and it will cause the histogram to rise up either the left side [underexposure] or the right side [overexposure] of the graph.

▶ *Recovery* is a cool feature which, when used in moderation, can 'bring back' lost highlights.

▶ *Fill Light* helps to open up deep shadows. Do not abuse this tool as it can result in very noisy images. I tend not to go over 25. There are other techniques for optimizing shadows and highlights and we have covered one in the 'Shadow/Highlights' tool exercise on page 168.

▶ *Blacks* controls deep shadows. Use this sparingly. If abused the histogram will soon tell you as it will start to rise up the left side of the

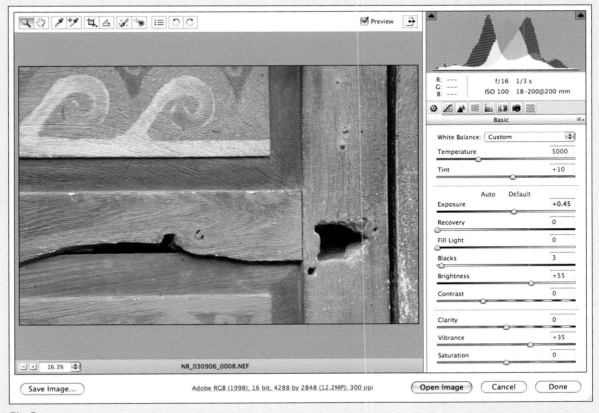

Fig 5

165

graph. You will find that you have more freedom to use this tool the flatter an image is.

▸ *Brightness* controls only the midtones in an image, unlike the Brightness tool in Photoshop, which makes a global adjustment.

▸ *Contrast* is another setting which should be used sparingly. I like to make the final tonal adjustments with 'Curves' once the image is open in Photoshop [Fig 8].

▸ *Clarity* helps to give the image more 'pop' by adjusting the edge transitions. Again, I use this option sparingly as I prefer the 'Curves' option in Photoshop.

▸ *Vibrance* is quite nice in some situations. It intensifies colors rather like the saturation tool but in a more subtle way. Used carefully it can help some images — make sure you keep an eye on the histogram as over adjustment will cause clipping.

▸ *Saturation* is one of the most abused tools out there. I have seen images that have had too much saturation applied — colors start to flatten, fine detail is lost, and more importantly, when you look at the histogram it is often 'off the chart', usually clipped in the shadows and often in the highlights as well. If you have to use the saturation tool I would recommend using it in Photoshop, and then only selectively on those colors which you feel need boosting. Remember though, if used carefully, the 'Curves' option in Photoshop is most often all an image needs.

PROCESSING THE FILE

Now to our image. On first inspection it is quite flat. The histogram shows that there is little shadow detail and little highlight detail. The majority of the information is concentrated in the middle of the graph backing up our initial assess-

ment of flatness [Fig 6]. Happy with the color temperature, my first move is to increase the exposure to open up the highlights [note the difference between Fig 1 and Fig 5]. I increase the 'Black' value until the histogram falls short of

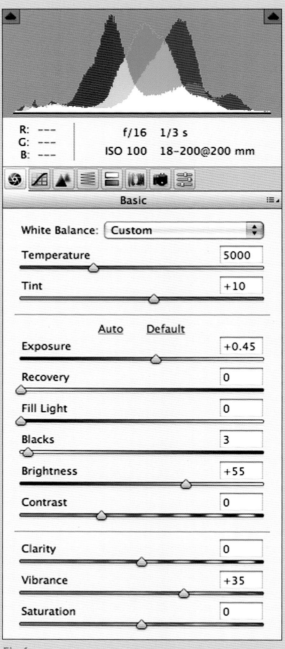

Fig 6

clipping. Then, to open up the image still further, I shift the 'Brightness' towards the highlight end of the scale until the average mass of peaks in the histogram is more in the center of the scale. Lastly, I add some 'Vibrance'. With these adjustments made, and with a histogram indicating that there are no exposure problems, I open the image. The next step is to check 'Levels' [Fig 7] to make sure there is no clipping, and finally an adjustment in 'Curves' [Fig 8] helps to increase contrast and boost the intensity of the colors. Then, I check for dust and save the image.

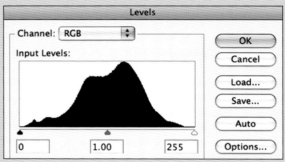

Fig 7

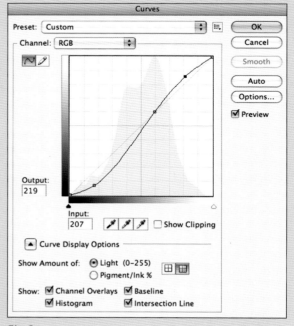

Fig 8

2. *Shadow / Highlights Tool* by Ray Klass

The 'Shadow/Highlights' tool is geared towards images that are correctly exposed [such as the image above], but that were taken under high-contrast conditions, and have lost some of the life in either the highlights or shadows, or both. By darkening the highlights, or lightening the shadows, the details within these areas are brought out, and the color saturation is improved.

What differentiates this tool from using 'Levels' or 'Curves' is that the correction can be limited to a specific tonal range. In other words, the user can control what Photoshop considers to be a shadow or a highlight, and exactly how much lightening or darkening is applied to that area. This powerful adjustment feature works much faster than using selections or masks.

To begin with, open the image in Photoshop [Adobe Camera RAW for RAW files], and then adjust the sliders so that all of the detail is preserved [Fig 1]. By this, I mean that the histogram extends to both the shadow and highlight sides of the graph, rather than going off the end of the scale. Also, the triangle above the highlight and shadow sides should be black. This means that your image has maintained its detail from black to white.

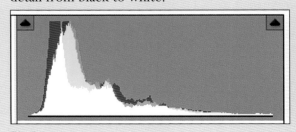

Fig 1

It may not be possible, even with the adjustments in camera RAW, to obtain this ideal histogram. At that point, it is important to look at which areas are losing detail, and make a decision as to whether it is really critical detail that is missing. The 'Shadow/Highlights' tool will not create detail where there is none, rather it works on the available detail to improve the tonality of these areas.

Once these settings are adjusted, it is time to open the image in Photoshop by clicking the 'Open Image' button at the bottom right of the Adobe Camera RAW box. With the image open, make any general tonal and color adjustments that you would normally do ['Levels', 'Curves', etc].

With the general adjustments completed, it is time to start the targeted manipulation of the image with the 'Shadow/Highlights' tool. From the screen menu select Image>Adjustments> Shadow/Highlights to access the tool [Fig 2].

Fig 2

Initially, you may have a box that appears with only the basic options, if this is the case, click on 'Show More Options' [Fig 3]. This reveals the more helpful and precise controls that really enable you to target specific tonal ranges with this tool [Fig 4]. You will notice that the dialog box is broken down into three basic sections, 'Shadows', 'Highlights', and 'Adjustments'. The 'Shadows' and 'Highlights' sections both have identical sliders that deal with the tones in either the shadows or the highlights. The 'Adjustments' section deals with general corrections that affect both the highlights and shadows.

This tool works by selectively darkening the highlights, and lightening the shadows. Looking at both the 'Shadows' and 'Highlights' sections, there are three identical sliders, 'Amount', 'Tonal Width', and 'Radius'. The first slider, 'Amount', is asking how much lightening or darkening should be applied.

The second slider, 'Tonal Width' is asking which areas Photoshop should consider to be a shadow, or consider to be a highlight. Photoshop is looking, pixel-by-pixel, at the entire image and judging, based on tone, whether a specific area should be considered a highlight or shadow, or somewhere in-between. This slider is your way of targeting specific tonal ranges.

The last slider, 'Radius', is asking how you want to handle the transition area between what Photoshop is lightening or darkening, and the areas that are not being affected at all. The further to the right this slider is, the larger the transition area, and the softer the transition will be. In effect you're hiding the tonal manipulation with this slider.

There's an easy, step-by-step method to adjusting these sliders. I first adjust the three in the 'Shadows' box, and then adjust the other three in the 'Highlights' box, using the same technique for both sets.

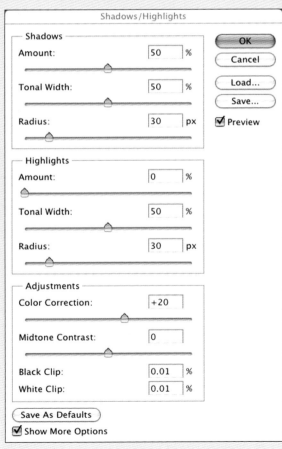

Fig 4

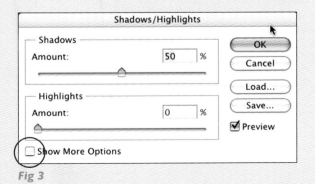

Fig 3

AMOUNT

First, set the 'Amount' slider to 100%. You are sliding it all the way to the right so that the change [darkening for the 'Highlights' box, or lightening for the 'Shadows' box] is as pronounced as possible – this will make our next step of targeting the correct tonal areas much easier. You will later re-adjust this, so don't worry if it doesn't look good.

TONAL WIDTH

Second, set the 'Tonal Width' slider to 0%. Then slide the 'Tonal Width' to the right, watching the preview of the image to see what area Photoshop is affecting. As you slide from left to right, Photoshop will begin to consider more and more areas either as shadows or highlights. You are watching for the moment when Photoshop is affecting only the areas you want to lighten or darken, and none of the other areas.

Once you have the 'Tonal Width' set, go back and re-examine the 'Amount' slider. You will most likely need to move it back toward the left to achieve your desired lightening or darkening.

RADIUS

With your 'Amount' slider set, it is time for the third and last slider, 'Radius'. This is used to control the transition between the areas Photoshop is working on, and those that it is not affecting. The greater the adjustment of the 'Amount' slider, the greater the radius will need to be to seamlessly blend the manipulation. I start by bringing the slider all the way to left. This will make the image look as though you were viewing it through a smudged piece of glass. Next, drag the slider to the right, looking for the point

169

'…the user can control what Photoshop considers to be a shadow or a highlight, and exactly how much lightening or darkening is applied to that area.'

where the image regains its detail. This indicates that the radius is large enough to hide the lightening or darkening effect.

I first use the above steps for the 'Shadows' box, and then repeat them for the 'Highlights' box. By no means are you required to do both the 'Highlights' and 'Shadows', some images may only need one or the other. In this case, simply set the sliders of the section you don't need to use to '0'.

With both the 'Shadows' and 'Highlights' set, I turn my attention to the 'Adjustments' section. Literally, the 'Shadow/Highlights' tool is making what was once dark, lighter, and what was once light, darker, so it stands to reason that if you've made some heavy adjustments you might lose some of the overall contrast in your image. The 'Color Correction' and 'Midtone Contrast' sliders are built to compensate for this. 'Color Correction' can either increase or reduce saturation – I adjust this by eye using a color-calibrated monitor. The second slider, 'Midtone Contrast' helps to put back some 'pop' in the midtones, and I also adjust this by eye [Fig 5].

In my experience, the last two settings, 'Black Clip' and 'White Clip' are just fine left at their default values – if you have processed the image carefully in Adobe Camera RAW, adjusting them makes almost no difference at all so I rarely, if ever do.

Finally, with all of my adjustments made, I use the 'Preview' checkbox [Fig 5] to get an idea of how I've changed the image, keeping in mind that if the result is not positive there may be further adjustments necessary. When I am completely satisfied, I click the 'OK' button, and save my image [right].

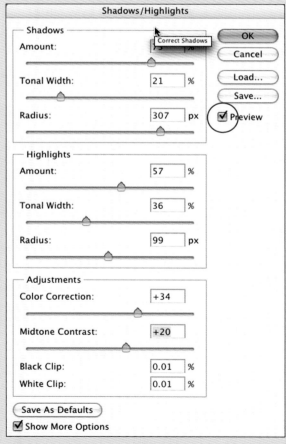

Fig 5

3.   *Lens Correction Filter*

As digital photography advances by quantum leaps, software manufacturers such as Adobe have kept pace with these advancements. The improved 'Lens Correction' filter in Photoshop CS3 is one that I use frequently when processing my images.

It was discovered during the digital transition that many of the lenses we had depended on in the film days did not really perform well when exposing onto a digital sensor. Consequently, many of these lenses have been redesigned and re-branded as 'digital' versions. Optics have been adjusted to compensate for flaws such as lack of critical edge sharpness and chromatic aberration.

Additionally, newer lenses have appeared giving the photographer the widest range of possibilities in a single piece of glass – for instance, the Canon 16-300mm. This is an amazing travel lens but the optical quality at certain focal lengths is questionable. Depending on how a lens such as this is used, other factors come in to play, like vignetting [at large apertures] and barrel distortion [at the wider end of the focal range].

The smart people at Adobe have come to the rescue and most of these problems can be resolved in seconds with simple slider controls in the 'Lens Correction' filter.

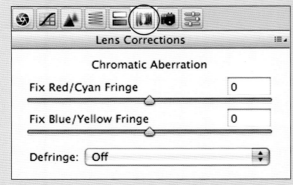

Fig I

Additionally, if you photograph architecture, and if you do not own a tilt/shift lens, the 'Transform' option in this filter has made it possible to intelligently correct keystoning, or perspective, at the same time as proportionally adjusting the relative height of the image.

Let us now look at the options available to us. To access this filter, open an image which needs to worked on and from the menu at the top of the screen select Filter>Distort>Lens Correction.

REMOVE DISTORTION

This slider adjusts for barrel distortion which is often caused by using a zoom lens with a wide range of focal lengths [eg. 16 - 300mm], more often apparent in the wide angle range

CHROMATIC ABERRATION

This occurs when light entering the lens begins to refract or split from white sunlight into the colors of the spectrum. This phenomenon is a particularly visible at the edge of the frame when using ultrawide lenses such as a 16-35mm, and

Fig 2

primarily on images taken on full frame sensors. Although traditionally camera manufacturers have made efforts to reduce this chromatic aberration with the use of low-dispersion glass, it has not been eliminated completely.

If you shoot JPGs you will make these adjustments in the 'Lens Correction' filter. If you shoot RAW the adjustments are made more efficiently in Adobe Camera RAW, which uses the same filter as part of its interface [choose the lens symbol third from the right Fig 1]. For the sake of this exercise I will make the Chromatic Aberration adjustments in the Lens Correction filter in Photoshop since the steps are identical.

Open an image which has been taken with a wide angle lens and examine the edges at 100% on the screen. Look at any hard edges and chances are you will see either a red/cyan or a blue/yellow shift [Fig 2]. Open the 'Lens Correction' filter Filter>Distort>Lens Correction. Under the heading 'Chromatic Aberration' you will see two sliders. Depending upon which colors which are separating adjust the relevant slider. In this case moving the Red/Cyan slider +8 to the right did the job [Fig 3].

PERSPECTIVE CONTROL

When photographing architecture, I like to keep my verticals straight, where possible, to avoid convergence [or keystoning]. To achieve this the

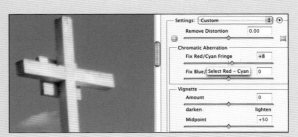

Fig 3

camera has to be as level as possible, and depending on the height of the structure will dictate how much foreground you will have to have to achieve the parallel verticals. Another way to achieve this is to get yourself into an elevated location thereby reducing the amount of foreground. If this is not possible, and you do not have an interesting foreground, the next option is to tilt the camera upwards until you have the composition you want. The 'Lens Correction' will help you reduce the convergence, depending on how radical the tilt is.

In this example [Fig 4], I am looking up at the window, and I am as far from it as I can be to reduce the angle of tilt. Some convergence is evident, and there is some barrel distortion in the lintel above the window and on the building trim at the top of the frame.

I open the 'Lens Correction' filter Filter> Distort>Lens Correction. Before making any further adjustments I make sure that the image is vertical in the center of the frame so that the perspective adjustments will be applied equally to each side. I do this by using the ruler tool which is the second icon down on the left side of the 'Lens Correction' window [Fig 5]. I find a straight edge in the middle of the frame and drag the ruler down that line. The image straightens automatically. If needed I fine-tune rotation with the 'Angle' wheel [it easier to enter values into the box than to physically rotate the wheel].

I make my changes [Fig 5], with the help of the useful icons which give me an idea in which direction to move the sliders [the image proportions will change so if you need to see all of your image adjust the 'Scale' slider at the bottom of the window until the complete image is in the frame]. Changes are updated immediately in the preview window. I open the image, retouch, recrop and then save [Fig 6 overleaf].

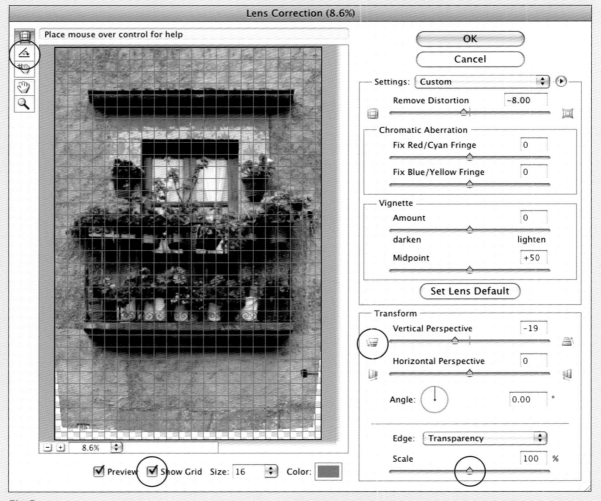

Fig 4

Fig 5

Fig 6

VIGNETTE

Another option available in the 'Lens Correction' filter is the 'Vignette' slider. This is a particularly useful tool if you are photographing with a wide open aperture and you are unable to stop down due to the need for a fast shutter speed. Depending on the quality of the lens, using a large aperture will result in fall-off towards the corners of the image, otherwise known as vignetting.

The 'Vignette' slider [Fig 7] attemps to fix this problem, and it does so quite successfully. The first slider darkens or lightens the corners and the one below it controls the intensity of the effect by controlling how close to the center of the frame the gradation starts.

This could also be a useful tool for portrait photographers who like to 'burn-in' their corners, an effect they used to do in the darkroom by using cut-out cardboard masks.

OTHER CONTROLS

There are a couple of other things worth mentioning such as the grid, which can be turned on and off, and which is useful for aiding in the straightening of images. The control pallette at the top left side of the window [Fig 5] includes inter-active control of 'Distortion' and 'Angle', and the option to move the grid with the hand/grid tool. As always in Photoshop, the best way to discover these functions and to determine whether they will fit into your workflow is to experiment on a wide range of images.

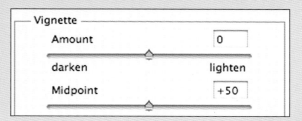

Fig 7

Although this image of an amazingly elaborate 'Day of the Dead' altar was taken from ground-level, with the camera pointing upwards, it was possible to effectively correct the convergence using the 'Lens Correction' filter.

4. *Black & White Tool*

The Black & White image adjustment feature is a very cool tool. It helps you turn a color image into a grayscale image, and it allows complete control of the process by allowing you to fine-tune your adjustments according to the colors and tones in the original color photograph.

The image I have chosen is interesting in that it contains reds, blues and greens, and depending on which color sliders we use in the conversion process we will be able to see a profound effect on each of these colors.

To find the Black & White adjustment tool go to the menu at the top of the screen and select Image>Adjustments>Black and White [Fig 1].

A dialog box will appear giving you the conversion options. On first opening, Photoshop

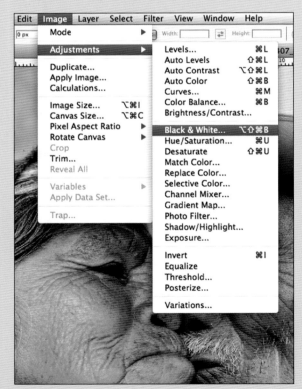

Fig 1

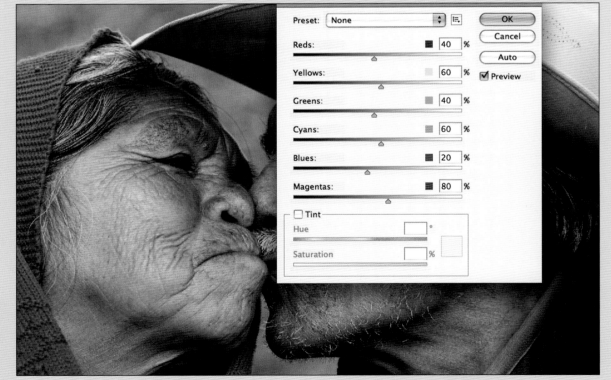

Fig 2

will make an intelligent guess [Fig 2] whereupon you can make your own adjustments.

What I like to do is to set all of the color sliders to zero and then, one by one, by moving each in turn to the left and the right, I can ascertain what effect [if any] each color slider has on the image. In many cases one or more of the sliders will remain on zero as they do not have any useful effect on the overall image.

Before I proceed with describing the adjustments I made in this image please be warned not to overdo the effect. Make sure that you do not plug up your shadows [I always keep the 'Histogram' (Fig 3) and the 'Info' (Fig 4) windows on the screen to make sure the image is not clipping]. Try to keep the deepest shadows in the range of '5 - 13' but no lower [Fig 4].

Once I have zeroed each of the sliders, I start by moving the red slider first. It is instantly obvious that as I move the slider into the negative territory the woman's shawl goes too dark so I opt to leave the red at zero for now.

The next slider, the yellow, enables me to control the green/yellow background, so I set this at '40', darkening it, but still giving me good separation between my subjects.

The green slider makes little difference to the background so I opt to leave it at '0'.

Adjusting the cyan gives me good control over

the man's shirt allowing me to achieve good separation between his skin and his dark sweater.

The blue slider altered a different range of tones in the blue shirt so I put it in positive territory until I was pleased with the result.

The magenta slider gives me the most dramatic effect by lightening the woman's shawl without causing it to go too flat. It has the effect of building up contrast whereas when I try a similar adjustment with the red slider it has the effect of lightening the shawl too evenly. After getting the magenta slider where I need it I go back to the red and slide it to '-5' darkening the shawl slightly but making sure that I do not block up the shadows [Fig 5].

If your monitor is well calibrated you should be able to control these adjustments very accurately. As in every situation, where color or tone is involved, it becomes very subjective so my recommendation is to experiment with a variety of images – those with a wide range of colors, extreme tonal variations, images of people, both light-skinned and dark-skinned – you will be blown away by the effects you can achieve.

Once you have made your black and white conversion you can save the settings as a preset for future use by clicking on the small box to the right of the Preset pop-up menu [Fig 5]. Select 'Save Preset…', name it, and save it in the default

Black and White folder. The next time you want to access it select the same small box to the right of the preset pop-up menu and select 'Load Preset…' and choose the option from the list of your saved preset values.

Photoshop provides a selection of its own preset values loosely based on traditional black & white filters that photographers used to use when photographing with black & white negative film. While some will not give you what you are looking for, others will give you a good starting point, from which you can then make your own finer adjustments.

Finally, this adjustment tool allows you to color your black and white images. If you select the 'Tint' box at the bottom of the screen it will open up the 'Hue' and 'Saturation' sliders. The 'Hue' slider gives the image the color so, for example, if you like a sepia tone, set 'Hue' on 40 and 'Saturation' on 5. Again, as always experiment, and be warned that your shadows may begin to plug up so use this option with great care!

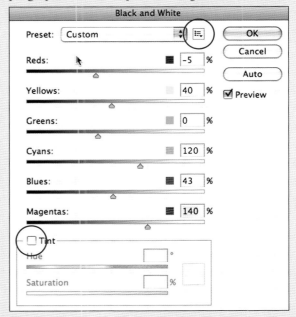

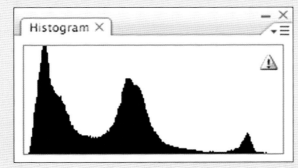

Fig 3

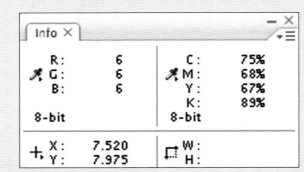

Fig 4

Fig 5

ACKNOWLEDGEMENTS

*T*hank you to my family and friends who have understood the importance of loving encouragement, and to my extended workshop family, who regularly show up and accept my dance invitations with generous spirit. You are the wind beneath my wings.

With respect and admiration, I dedicate this book to the wives, lovers, and daughters of the soldiers who fought in the Mexican Revolution. The names of many of these women, known as *las soldaderas*, have been forgotten or omitted from history books. Fearless, *las soldaderas* were valiant in their quest to regain and preserve their rights against a multitude of social injustices. Through their bravery, these women soldiers broke the mould of countless generations and paved the way for Mexican women for generations to come.

I dedicate this book to all the ordinary people in the world who when told that they were the underdogs, did not internalize that assumption. Instead, they discovered the courage to raise their voices in reclamation of themselves. I dedicate this book to the celebration of heroic cries everywhere, as they stand firmly in their own battlefields, living boldly, pursuing a meaningful life in which they are able to sing their song and with heart and spirit — create their dance — *Nancy Rotenberg, Sept 2008*

I dedicate this book to my wife Nicole who has kept the home fires burning during my frequent absences, and who has always encouraged me to 'do a book' — well, finally, here it is; and to my son Callum whose journey is just beginning.

Thanks to Luis Miguel López Alanís for his Brief History of San Miguel de Allende, and for being a great guide on our trip to Michoacán; to Ray Klass for writing the 'Shadow/Highlights'

tool exercise in the Digital Techniques section. Thanks to my father and to Marian Moore for casting their eagle eyes over the text, and to Dee Whittlesey for her Texas hospitality.

I am grateful to the many people who have allowed me onto their roofs, into their homes, hotels and places of worship, so that I could capture those special views, which for me, captured the essence of San Miguel. To *La Posadita* restaurant for always making space on their rooftop terrace for our large groups — and for serving the best *guacamole*!

Special thanks must go to Diane Kushner for providing restful haven for our photographers, John & Diane Patience for letting me photograph in their home and on their terrace [WOW, what a view], Andrea Flores, *gracias*, Marilyn Sibley and Beatriz Orvañanos for helping me produce my lifestyle shoots, my models, and most especially to the people of San Miguel who have allowed us to intrude in their lives and capture a sense of place. *Abrazos a todos!*

Finally, to my workshop partner, Nancy, a big thank you for helping me to see a little more with my heart, and to all of the people who have been on our workshops. Thanks for sharing!

— *Jeremy Woodhouse, Sept 2008*

▲ Las Soldaderas — *photographed during one of the countless parades and celebrations through the streets of San Miguel.*

'Ring the bells that still can ring
Forget your perfect offering
There is a crack, a crack in everything
That's how the light gets in.'

Leonard Cohen